THROUGH

GOOD

AND

THROUGH
Prayers for a
GOOD TIMES
Lifetime Together
AND BAD

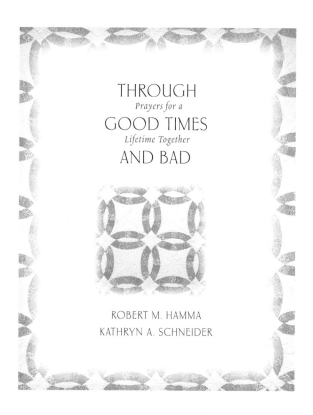

ROBERT M. HAMMA
KATHRYN A. SCHNEIDER

 SORIN BOOKS   Notre Dame, IN

Through Good Times and Bad

Presented to

Jana + Jack

by

Judy

on the occasion of

Christmas

on

_2001_

© 2000 by Sorin Books

All rights reserved. No part of this book may be used or reproduced in any manner whatsoever, except in the case of reprints in the context of reviews, without written permission from Sorin Books, P.O. Box 1006, Notre Dame, IN 46556-1006.

International Standard Book Number 1-893732-11-8

Library of Congress Catalog Card Number: 99-066889

Cover and text design by Katherine Robinson Coleman.

Printed and bound in the United States of America.

Quilts by: Christine Deithchley 32, 40-41; Renee S. Miller 27, 28-29, 35, 38-39, 42, 44, 47, 53, 56, 63, 78, 86; Dora Teagarden Robinson 82; Courtesy of St. Margaret's House 22, 24-25, 31, 48-49, 59, 66, 68, 72, 88-89.

ACKNOWLEDGMENTS

We want to thank everyone who helped us make this book a reality: our publisher Frank Cunningham and our editors John Kirvan and Julie Hahnenberg, who provided expert guidance and encouragement; Kristen Coney and Kathy Coleman for their beautiful design and all who supplied the quilts used in the design; our many friends at Sorin Books who reviewed the proposal and offered excellent suggestions of particular prayers to include; Kate Hermann, who read the manuscript as it developed and offered many helpful suggestions; Lois Davitz, who helped us find the Jewish wedding ceremony; and Chris Tessarowicz for her constant love and support. And of course we are grateful to our children, Peter, Christine, and Sarah, who give us so much love and enrich our marriage.

CONTENTS

INTRODUCTION ∾ 11

SACRED SIGNS, HOLY WORDS ∾ 17

NOURISHED BY THE WORD ∾ 23

THROUGH THE YEAR TOGETHER ∾ 33

PRAYERS FOR JOYFUL TIMES ∾ 45

PRAYERS FOR DIFFICULT TIMES ∾ 57

PARENTING ∾ 67

ROOTED AND GROUNDED IN LOVE ∾ 79

INDEX ∾ 91

Of the many gifts God has given you, one of the greatest is your spouse. Your husband or wife has pledged to love you in good times and in bad, in sickness and in health—come what may. Such a promise is one of the most wonderful gifts anyone could receive.

This love is not only a gift from God, but is a gift of God's own self. It is not really an exaggeration to say that the love of your spouse embodies God's love for you. St. John tells us, "God is love, and those who abide in love abide in God, and God abides in them" (1 John 4:16). Through the love of your spouse, God not only touches you, God dwells in you.

Love, of course, is mutual. In marriage, you not only receive love, you also give it. Just as your spouse's love for you is permeated with God's presence, so is your return of love. This daily give and take of your love is indeed a spiritual journey. Sharing of life and love with your partner is an integral part of your path to God.

There is nothing in a marriage more important than the gift of self exchanged between two people. One of the most beautiful prayers of the Catholic marriage rite says, "Love is our origin, love is our constant calling, love is our fulfillment in heaven." There is no substitute for this selfless love. St. Paul said as much when he wrote, "If I speak in the tongues of mortals and of angels, but do not have love, I am a noisy gong or a clanging cymbal. And if I have prophetic powers, and understand all mysteries and all knowledge, and if I have all faith, so as to remove mountains, but do not have love, I am nothing" (1 Corinthians 13:1-2). While Paul is not specifically referring to marriage, his words, so often read at weddings today, apply well in marriage.

While such thoughts may provide the inspiration we sometimes need, they do not replace the hard work that a marriage can often involve. Patience, understanding, sacrifice, and forgiveness are the practical ways that we both give and receive love in marriage. Developing true and lasting intimacy can be a difficult task at times. It requires a delicate balance between security and freedom, holding on and letting go.

Building this kind of relationship involves daily acts of love, but also prayer. Sometimes, because of our background or past experience, we can have a narrow notion of what prayer is. We may think of prayer only in terms of recitation of traditional prayers or participation in formal worship. Or we may pray only in times of difficulty or tragedy. While such prayer is indeed important, prayer can also be personal and spontaneous, and it can occur in joyful times as well as difficult times. Sometimes prayer is addressed directly to God, but sometimes it can be a reflective exercise where we begin by talking to ourselves or thinking about our spouse, and then are led, without noticing it, to speak to God. Many of the prayers in this collection reflect that movement.

The prayers in this book are written for a wide variety of experiences—from gratitude for the thoughtfulness of your spouse to difficulty with in-laws. They invite you to hearken back to the inspired words of scripture and the sacred actions of your wedding and call you to move forward on your journey together, whether you are in your first or fiftieth year together. They can serve to prime the pump of your own personal expression of prayer, or simply to gather together the fragments of your inner thoughts and reflections.

Hopefully, they will deepen your awareness of the sacred dimension that is present in every aspect of your life together. God can speak to us through the words of love that we say to each other, and also through the ordinary exchanges of information that we make every day. God can touch us through the tenderness and compassion of our spouse, and also through illness or personal upheaval. Prayer can often be a way of seeing things differently, of perceiving realities that lie below the surface of our lives and would otherwise go unnoticed.

As we have lived out our marriage within the Catholic tradition for fifteen years, we have come to appreciate more and more the emphasis our tradition places on marriage as a spiritual reality and as a path to God. But this appreciation of marriage is by no means unique to Catholicism or Christianity. All the world's religions share this awareness of marriage as a sacred reality where God is encountered and where God communicates to us through one another. This awareness has helped us to keep our perspective when problems confront us, and to appreciate the hidden beauty of each moment in our marriage. We hope that these prayers will help you within the context of your own religious tradition or personal search for faith to develop the habit of seeing your marriage from a spiritual perspective too.

SACRED
SIGNS,
HOLY
WORDS

Lord, you were with us
in that sacred moment
when we stood before family and friends,
looked into each other's eyes,
and said these words:

"I promise to be true to you
in good times and in bad,
in sickness and in health.
I will love you and honor you
all the days of my life."

By these words, Lord, you joined us together.
Write them now, O God of Faithfulness,
in our minds and in our hearts.
May they sustain us through the years,
may they keep us together
no matter what comes our way,
and may they inspire us to be generous,
patient, and forgiving to one another.

Amen.

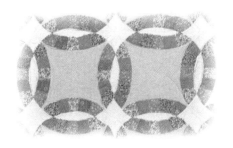

OUR RINGS

Lord, I look at my ring and I remember
the day we picked it out together,
the excitement of showing it to my family and friends,
the gentle way my spouse placed it on my finger for
the first time.
As you blessed our rings on the day of our wedding,
continue to bless us now.
Make them a lasting symbol of our deep faith in
each other,
a reminder of our hopes for the future,
and a sign of the love and commitment we share.

Amen.

Loving God, as you blessed us on the day of our
wedding,
may your blessing be upon us today.
Open our eyes
to see in each other the image and likeness of you,
our Creator.
Open our ears
to hear in each other's voice, your voice,
our gentle Shepherd.
Open our hands
to receive the gift of your healing touch,
our guiding Spirit.

May the sharing of our minds
bring us to know and understand each other
more deeply.
May the union of our hearts
help us to trust each other with our joys and our sorrows.
May the joining of our bodies
make us one in heart and mind.
Bless us, O Father, Son, and Holy Spirit.
Keep us faithful, generous, and kind,
one, as you are one.

God of Love,
with grateful hearts we look
back on our wedding ceremony
when we pledged that our two lives
would now become one.

Our wedding candle reminds us of our vow.
It reminds us that our life together
is guided by the light of your love.

Help us to remain always as one.
Illuminate our lives with your love.
If ever we lose our way, rekindle in us
the flame of faith, hope, and love.

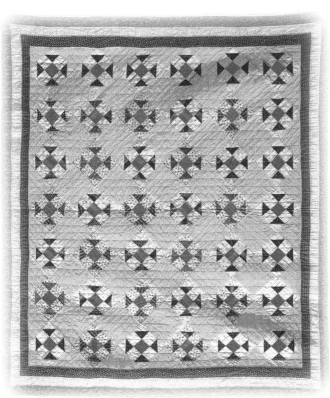

NOURISHED
BY
THE
WORD

Wherever you go, I will go,
wherever you live, I will live.
Your people shall be my people,
and your God, my God.

—Ruth 1:16

Gracious God,
growing up, we had separate lives,
our own dreams, our own homes,
and our own roads to travel.

Marriage has joined our separate lives and made us one.
We now share our dreams, our home,
and we travel a single road together.

Make us faithful, patient, and loving companions.
Give us a loving imagination to dream dreams
that will make a positive difference
in both our lives and the world we share.

Give us the gift of hospitality so that our home will be a
haven for friends and family.
And make the road we travel be one of love and peace.
May we be faithful disciples and a sign of your
love in this world.
Be with us always.

Let us love one another
since love comes from God
and everyone who loves
is begotten by God
and knows God.

—1 John 4:7

Gracious God,
you are the source of all love.
Your love is without condition and beyond measure.
Nothing we have done in the past
or will do in the future
merits your love for us.
It is a gift which gives us life.

Through the love we have for one another,
we glimpse the depth and the breadth of your love.
Perfect this love in us.

Make us generous, kind, and forgiving.
Help us to be faithful,
to love without condition and beyond measure,
to love as you love.

Allow your love to flow through us
as we reach out to others
so that we may be a faithful sign
of your love in this world today.

LOVE DOES NOT END

Love is always patient and kind;
it is never jealous;
love is never boastful or conceited;
it is never rude or selfish,
it does not take offense, and is not resentful.
Love takes no pleasure in other people's sins
but delights in the truth;
it is always ready to excuse, to trust, to hope,
and to endure whatever comes.
Love does not come to an end.

—1 Corinthians 13:4-8

Loving God,
you teach us how we should love one another.
On our best days, when we are fully in touch with our love
for each other,
we feel like we can love in this way.
Yet too often we fall short of the mark.

Write this law of love on our hearts.
Inspire us to be patient and kind.
Help us to leave jealousy, rudeness, conceit,
selfishness, and resentment behind.
Awaken us to perceive and delight in the truth.
Give us the capacity to be generous, forgiving, and trusting.

With your help, we will be able to endure whatever comes,
and we will live in the love that never ends.

For I am certain of this: neither death nor life,
no angel, no prince,
nothing that exists, nothing still to come,
not any power,
or height or depth, nor any created thing,
can ever come between us
and the love of God
made visible in Christ Jesus our Lord.

—Romans 8:38-39

All loving God,
the road which we have chosen to travel together
lies before us.
We know this road will take
us to the mountaintops of happiness and joy,
through lush forests of peace and contentment,
across fields which seem ordinary and mundane,
and down into valleys filled with pain and sorrow.

The wonder of it all is that we travel this road together
with you as our companion and guide.

Help us on our journey.
Make our path clear, our footing sure.
Help us be ever aware of your steadfast love for us.
Emblazon on our hearts the promise that nothing,
neither joy nor sorrow,
power nor weakness,
will ever come between our love for one another
and your love for us
made visible in Christ Jesus our Lord.

THROUGH

THE

YEAR

TOGETHER

Lord, you have promised
that wherever two or three are gathered in your name
you would be present in their midst.
We gather now in your name
and ask you to bless this place.
We thank you for the excitement we feel
as we begin our life here.
We are grateful to be able to have a place of our own,
and we remember all those who are without shelter.

As we begin our life here,
we pray for the gift of hospitality
to welcome others joyfully into our home.
We ask for the grace of awareness
to be mindful of all the gifts you have given us.
We ask for the patience we will need
as we work to make our hopes and dreams unfold.

May we always remember that you are our true home,
and that in the shelter of each other's hearts
we will be secure.
And so, dear God, bless our home
in the name of the Father, and of the Son,
and of the Holy Spirit.

Amen.

Gracious God, we thank you for this special night
when we celebrate (name the occasion).
We know that you are with us always
and that your Spirit is always at work in us.
Tonight we are grateful for the joy we share
on this happy occasion.
We thank you, too, for this meal before us.
Bless this food and bless all of us.
Give us a spirit of gratitude for all your gifts,
and for all the ways you are at work in our lives.
We ask this in faith and trust.

Amen.

All loving God,
we have so much to be grateful for today.
We thank you for the love that we share,
for our life together, and for our home.
We are grateful for all those whose love and support
have carried us through
the many changes of this past year.
As we remember all of these gifts,
keep us mindful too of all those who are less fortunate,
the hungry, the homeless, and the lonely.
Bless this wonderful meal
and all of us who share it.

Amen.

Lord, Jesus Christ,
as we celebrate your birth,
we thank you for coming among us
as God's very Word made flesh.
May the joy of this Christmas together,
the gifts we share, and the excitement of this day
remind us that you are with us still,
God's Word made flesh,
in the passionate exchange of our love
and in the simple ways we affirm and support each other.
Draw into the circle of our love
all those with whom we share this day,
especially those in need of a gentle, caring presence.

Amen.

BLESSING THE NEW YEAR

As the old year ends and the new begins,
we thank you for the gift of time together,
and for this year in which so much has begun.
May the love between us,
already familiar and yet unknown,
both surprise and challenge us in the year ahead.
With each new day,
may we be responsive to each other's needs.
With each new season,
may we recognize the mystery
of your presence among us.

God of all time,
may this be the first of many days in this new year
in which we recommit ourselves
to grow in our love,
and to share our unique gifts
with those you place in our lives.

As we begin this season of Lent,
let it be a time of renewal for us.
Help us to follow you, Lord,
no longer alone, but together.
Teach us how to share our faith,
to carry one another's burdens,
and to live in your presence each day.
May our fasting be from selfishness,
our prayer be for a forgiving heart,
and our charity be freely given
to each other and to those in need.
Let us follow you together, Lord,
for you are the source of our life and our love.

EASTER

On this Easter day
when we celebrate the gift of new life
we praise and thank you, risen Jesus, for being with us.
You revealed yourself to the two disciples
as they walked on the road to Emmaus.
Let us see you anew
as we walk hand in hand
and remember all that you have told us.
As we break bread and share a cup of wine together,
may we be signs of your presence in our world.
May those whom we touch feel the comfort of
your Spirit,
and may our life together point to the Creator of all life.

Can it be possible that another year has gone by?
A year of joy, a year of discovery, a year of change.

There is so much to be thankful for,
so many moments shared together,
so much love and support from family and friends.
Thank you, God, for your presence in it all.

There is so much to pray for,
so many uncertain steps taken,
so much that is fragile that needs to grow strong.
Help us, God, for without you we falter.

There is so much to celebrate,
as we remember our wedding
and the joy of that moment,
as we dream of a future that we've only begun.
Dance with us, Lord, as we rejoice in your love.

A year has gone by, a wonderful year
of joy and discovery and change!

PRAYERS
FOR
JOYFUL
TIMES

I thought I knew you, my love,
and yet I find there is so much more to know:
interests, abilities, possibilities I had never considered,
surprising moments when your love touches me in
unexpected ways.

I thank you, God, for the gift of my beloved,
whose love comes from you
and leads me back to you.
It is a mystery to me, this love . . .
familiar, wonderful beyond words,
yet unknown, full of unseen potential,
gentle, strong, comfortable, challenging.
It beckons me insistently to follow,
to go further, to be more.

Let me delight in my beloved
who leads me to you in unexpected ways,
whose love enfolds me with your mysterious presence.

Like river and sea are we
mingled together, ebbing and flowing,
two made one, yet each still ourselves.

In the ecstasy of our union
we discover the mystery at the heart of our love,
the mystery at the heart of the world.

In giving, we receive,
in letting go, we are held tight,
in dying, we are born anew.

Praise to you, Maker of all love,
for the gift of our loving,
and for the way it immerses us in your mystery.

O river of life!
O ocean of goodness!

Sometimes I can scarcely believe
that you love me so much.
I wonder why.
How can this be?

You see my faults,
but you overlook them.
You know my foibles,   .
but you just smile at them.
You gaze at me, as if I were perfect.

No one has ever loved me like this.
I am amazed,
elated,
even giddy when I think about it.

How can I ever thank you, O God,
for placing such love in my life?
It was you who knew me before I was born
and chose for me such a wonderful partner.

It was you who brought us together
from our separate paths
and gave us the gift of each other.

Teach me to love
as I am loved,
as you love me.
Teach me to hold
this gift in my hands
gently, firmly.

You surprise me, Lord,
when you touch me unexpectedly
with the hand of my beloved.

You comfort me, my Shepherd,
when you speak reassuringly
through the voice of my true spouse.

You strengthen me, my Friend,
when you look upon me knowingly
through the eyes of my companion.

You inspire me, O Holy One,
when you breathe your life so gently
through the breath of my dear love.

You guide my steps, O Dancer,
as you urge me on so gracefully
through the leading of my partner.

May I find you each day anew
in the presence of my spouse.

When I think of the friends
who enrich our life
I am so grateful.

Their encouragement has helped us
to get where we are today,
to be together.

Their laughter makes us laugh
and remember all the good times we've had
and all we look forward to.

Their support has carried us
when things were tough
and we couldn't make it on our own.

Thank you, Lord, for the friends in our lives,
each one is a reflection of you.
Teach us to blend our unique gifts together
so that we can deepen our old friendships
and be open to new ones.

For the gift of life,
nurturing care through childhood,
guidance across turbulent years,
and support in our new life together,
for all this and so much more, Lord,
we are grateful to our families.

Thank you for the gift of our parents,
our siblings, our relatives.
They have been with each of us
in good times and in bad,
in sickness and in health.
Sometimes their love was "for better,"
sometimes it seemed "for worse."
And though we are now apart from them,
they are with us still.

So much of what we love in each other
is a reflection of them,
and some of what we struggle with
comes from them too.

Help us to imitate all the good they do,
and with your guidance,
may we take what they have given us
and build a home of our own.

Rooted firmly in their love,
may we grow strong according to your will,
and bear good fruit for the sake of your world.

FOR THE FRIENDSHIP OF MY SPOUSE

No one knows me the way you do.
No one understands me
or cares about me like you.

When I want to have fun or be serious,
or just hang out and relax,
there's no one I'd rather do it with than you.

You listen carefully to what I say.
You think about my feelings before your own.
You give me good advice when I ask for it.

You are my soul friend, God's best gift to me,
and I will always thank my God
for the light of friendship that shines in your eyes.

These little unexpected gifts
remind me that you care:
a call at work,
a thoughtful note,
a favor here and there.

They tell me that you carry me
with you throughout the day
in your mind
and in your heart
as you go along your way.

Do I take such things too lightly?
Do I remember you,
and imitate
your thoughtfulness
in what I say and do?

Now let us both remember Christ
who once washed Peter's feet.
And let us join
our hearts as one
where love and kindness meet.

PRAYERS
FOR
DIFFICULT
TIMES

I am angry, I am hurt, I am disappointed.
How could you say that?
Why did you do that?
Did you want to hurt me?
Did I want to hurt you?

Now there is a distance between us,
an emptiness that frightens me.
I want to turn away from it,
but when I run, it follows.

I do not know where to turn
and so I come to you, Lord.
Help me to find a way through that emptiness,
lead us back to each other.

Heal my wounds, calm my fears, give me comfort.
Teach me how to recognize my faults,
give me the strength to forgive
and the courage to ask for forgiveness.
You who brought us together,
be with us now.

This was not supposed to happen now!
"In sickness and in health . . ." yes,
but sickness only later,
much, much later,
after we've done all that we've planned,
after we've accomplished all that we're working for.

Lord, I don't understand this,
and you know I don't like it.
I'm afraid.
I feel helpless,
out of control,
guilty for being so caught up in myself.

Lord, I need you here with me.
I want you to take this away,
but if not,
then just let me know you are here.

Give us both the courage to face this.
Don't let us give up hope,
and teach us how to support each other.

Come, Lord Jesus, come.

It's the little things, Lord,
that are driving me crazy,
things I overlooked before,
things I never knew.

The differences between us
seem so small, even petty from a distance.
I'm not sure if I'm too picky,
or if I should give in.

Let me know when to voice my feelings,
and when to let them go.
Teach me not to bury issues
that must be faced right now.

Give me a forgiving spirit
and an understanding heart.
Help me to be more patient
and to remember that I'm not perfect.

Lord, I'm just so tired sometimes.
The pressure of work wears me out.
When I come home, I feel empty.
I just want to be left alone.
I need some space.

Help me not to take out my frustrations
on my spouse.
Teach me how to calm down
before I come home.
Preserve me from the quick word,
the cynical remark
that ruins what little is left
of our time together.

Give me perspective
on what's really important.
Help me to be aware
of what kind of life I'm choosing to create.
Don't let me forget
that the love between us
is more important
than anything else,
including my job.

Lord, how did we get into this mess?
It happened so quickly.
We seem to have lost control.
And the worst part
is when we blame each other.
The truth is, Lord,
that we are both at fault.

Help us to recognize our limits.
Give us patience to wait for what we want.
Help us to understand each other's attitudes
about money,
and the reasons why
we feel as we do.

Let us find our true joy
not in what we own,
or where we live,
but in the love we share
and in your presence with us.
You are our foundation.
May your spirit guide us.

WHEN WE'RE APART

What a wonderful gift you have given me.
I have found a home in you.
Even when we're apart,
I carry your love with me,
secure that it is always a part of me.

O God, help me always to be in touch with this love.
May it give me strength and confidence
as I negotiate the unknowns of travel.

Help us always to make our home in you.
Let us never be separated from your faithful love.
Bring us home safely to one another
and help us look confidently toward our eternal
home in you.

I hate getting lost!
I miss my friends!
There was a certainty about things in our old place,
at least I knew who I was and where I was.

Loving God,
we have chosen to come to this new place—
a new world, a new life, with new friends.
New possibilities lie ahead of us.
Open our eyes to all that is good before us.
Open our hearts to new friends.
Bless our new home.
Help us to be patient with ourselves
and with each other
during this time of transition.
Help us to find strength in one another and in you.

Lord, they are just so different from my family.
Give me patience.

When they are critical,
help me not to react.
When they seem resentful of me,
give me the strength to hold back.
When they tell me how to run my life,
let me just smile.

Where there is harshness,
may I sow kindness.
Where there is anger,
help me to put understanding.
Where there is hurt,
let me place forgiveness.

For the sake of my spouse,
whom I love so much,
teach me to accept them for who they are.
Open my eyes to see them as you do.
Let me some day
move beyond acceptance to appreciation
and, at last,
to love.

PARENTING

AN EXPECTANT MOTHER'S PRAYER

Creator of all life,
thank you for this precious gift.
The miracle of new life grows within me.
My heart leaps with joy and praise.
My mind trembles with awe and fear.

As this child grows within me,
help me to let go of the illusion of control
I once had over my body.
Help me to accept all the changes that are occurring.
Give to me a peaceful heart.
Help me to trust in all that is to come.
Be with me now.
My motherhood has already begun.

Lord, I still can't believe
that I am going to be a father,
that a new life is going to come
into the world
because of me.

I don't think I'm ready
for what this all means,
for the changes between us,
for this new responsibility.

Prepare me, Lord, for what is to come.
Help me support my wife
during her pregnancy.
Help me to be aware
of what she is going through.
Give me patience when I feel forgotten.
Give me courage to face so many challenges.

Thank you, God, for the gift of our child.
Let me treasure this gift.
Help me to care for him well,
to be a good father,
a good role model,
and a good husband.

Our child is born!
Thanks be to God!

This child is a miraculous sign of our love for one
another.
This child is a wondrous gift and sign of your love for us.

Grant us the wisdom we need
to teach her all that is good.
Grant us the eyes to see the best in her.
Grant us the ears to hear all she has to say,
especially the unspoken words.
Grant us hearts of unconditional love.
Grant us the hands of nurture and compassion.
Grant us the patience for all the trying times ahead.

For all that has been and all that will be
in our life with our newborn child,
we give you thanks and praise!

Creator of Life,
I'm in shock.
I thought we would have more time
for just the two of us to grow together,
to create a home before we had children.
I'm just learning what it means to be a wife.
Now the gift of a child has been given to us.
I must learn what it means to be a mother.
I'm afraid.

Come to me quickly.
Change my fear to confidence,
my uncertainty to joy.
Help me to accept this child as the wonderful,
beautiful miracle and gift that he is.
Be with me now and help me to realize that with your
help and steadfast love, all will be well.

A PARENT'S PRAYER

This child of ours is a mystery to me.
More than the sum of us two,
something like me,
something like you,
but mostly, someone new.

This unique person
who is growing every day
challenges me to pay attention,
to observe, to listen.

Usually I know what to expect.
I'm not easily taken in or surprised.
But when I get too settled in my parenting ways,
some surprising word or unforeseen act
reminds me not to take this gift for granted.

O Giver of Life and all good gifts,
thank you for the ways you draw me to yourself
through this child.
Help me to balance
speaking with listening,
correction with encouragement,
and holding on with letting go.

May your Holy Spirit
who dwells in us all
guide and protect us.

O God!
Hold us in your mercy,
in your compassion,
in your tender care.

Heal my child . . . your child.
Take away the pain,
take away the suffering,
take away the fear.
Take it all, Lord, it's too much for us.

Give me the strength not to falter,
give me the faith to know you are here,
give me the wisdom to choose the right treatments.

Stay with (your child's name),
be with all of our family,
and guide those who are caring for us.

Hold us in your gentle hands.

God, I'm exhausted.
Sometimes I just don't know what to do.
I'm trying my best,
but I can never keep up
with the demands,
with the arguments,
with the complaints,
with the rebellions.

Lord, help me to step back and take stock
of what is reasonable and what is not.
Teach me how to carve out space,
to renew my soul and refresh my spirit.
Help me to say "no" when I must,
and to give generously when I should.
Show me the way to rekindle the love in our family.
Help us all to be more tolerant, patient, and forgiving.

You are my strength,
I rely on you.

From the moment of your conception,
I loved you.
From the first time I held you,
I cherished you.
I never knew a love so fierce and deep existed.
It surprised me that this love was so different
from any other I had experienced.

Yet, it also surprised me that there,
around the edges of my joy,
lurked a feeling of sorrow.
Just a twinge at first.
I tried to push it away.
But it kept creeping back.
It puzzled me.

Then I knew.
The mourning had begun
for the day I would have to let go.

When I first understood,
the sorrow was as deep as the love,
for I imagined that somehow
I would lose you completely.

Now that time has passed.
We have both grown older and wiser.
I have learned that every day
presents a lesson for letting go.
There is some sorrow now,
but there is much more joy.
From the moment I first held you,
with love overwhelming,
I began my long good-bye.

Gracious God,
keep my cherished child under your protection
as she moves on to this new stage in her life.
Help us both to recognize that true love is eternal.

ROOTED
AND
GROUNDED
IN LOVE

For everything there is a season,
and a time for every matter under heaven:
a time to be born, and a time to die;
a time to plant, and a time to pluck up what is planted;
a time to kill, and a time to heal;
a time to break down, and a time to build up;
a time to weep, and a time to laugh;
a time to mourn, and a time to dance;
a time to throw away stones,
and a time to gather stones together;
a time to embrace,
and a time to refrain from embracing;
a time to seek, and a time to lose;
a time to keep, and a time to throw away;
a time to tear, and a time to sew;
a time to keep silence, and a time to speak;
a time to love, and a time to hate;
a time for war, and a time for peace.

—Ecclesiastes 3:1-8

The Lord is my shepherd, I shall not want.
    He makes me lie down in green pastures;
he leads me beside still waters;
    he restores my soul.
He leads me in right paths
    for his name's sake.

Even though I walk through the darkest valley,
    I fear no evil;
for you are with me;
    your rod and your staff—
    they comfort me.

You prepare a table before me
    in the presence of my enemies;
you anoint my head with oil;
    my cup overflows.
Surely goodness and mercy shall follow me
    all the days of my life,
and I shall dwell in the house of the Lord
    my whole life long.

Blessed are you, our God, Maker of the Universe!

And blessed are we who have come together
to walk as one
and to encircle each other
with loving kindness.

Blessed are we who partake together
in the cup of life,
sanctified by your commandments,
consecrated by the sharing of our rings.

Blessed are we who are fashioned
in the image of the Holy One,
whose favor gladdens our hearts
and brings intense joy to our souls.

Blessed are we who live
in the delight of our love
and bring true peace and companionship
to all we meet.

Blessed are you, our God, Maker of the Universe!

—Based on the Jewish Marriage Service

This then, is what I pray,
kneeling before the Father,
from whom every family in heaven and on earth
takes its name.
According to the riches of his glory
may he, through his Spirit,
enable your inner self to grow strong
so that Christ may dwell in your hearts through faith.
Then, rooted and grounded in love,
together with all of God's holy people,
may you have the power to comprehend
the breadth and length,
the height and depth of God's love.
May you thus know the love of Christ
which surpasses all knowledge,
and may you be filled with all the fullness of God.

To God,
who by the power of the Spirit at work within us,
is able to do far more than we can ask or imagine,
to him be glory,
in the church and in Christ Jesus to all generations,
for ever and ever. Amen.

(adapted from Ephesians 3:14-21)

Our Father,
Our Mother,
we reflect your image.
You are in heaven,
and here in our midst.
Hallowed be your name
in all we say and do together.

Your kingdom come
    in our home, in our family, in our work.
Your will be done
    in our bodies, in our hearts, in our minds.
On earth as it is in heaven,
    today and always.
Give us this day our daily bread,
    our daily strength, our daily renewal.
Forgive us our sins,
    our pettiness, our thoughtless ways,
As we forgive those who sin against us,
    each time with grace and gentleness.
And lead us not into temptation,
    down those roads that lead away from each other,
But deliver us from evil,
    within and around us.
For the kingdom, the power, and the glory are yours,
    now and forever. Amen.

YOU AND I

In that place we laugh ecstatically,
you and I.
What a miracle, you and I
   entwined in the same nest.
What a miracle, you and I
   one love, one lover, one Fire
in this world and the next,
in an ecstasy without end.

—Rumi

A MOMENT'S INDULGENCE

I ask for a moment's indulgence to sit by thy side.
The works that I have in hand
I will finish afterwards.

Away from the sight of thy face
my heart knows no rest or respite,
and my work becomes an endless toil
in a shoreless sea of toil.

Today the summer has come at my window
with its sighs and murmurs;
and the bees are plying their minstrelsy
at the court of the flowering grove.

Now it is time to sit quiet
face to face with thee,
and to sing dedication of life
in this silent and overflowing leisure.

—Rabindranath Tagore

HOW DO I LOVE THEE?

How do I love thee? Let me count the ways.
I love thee to the depth and breadth and height
My soul can reach, when feeling out of sight
For the ends of Being and ideal Grace.
I love thee to the level of every day's
Most quiet need, by sun and candlelight.
I love thee freely, as men strive for Right;
I love thee purely, as they turn from Praise.

I love with a passion put to use
In my old griefs, and with my childhood's faith.
I love thee with a love I seemed to lose
With my lost saints,—I love thee with the breath,
Smiles, tears, of all my life!—and, if God choose,
I shall but love thee better after death.

—Elizabeth Barrett Browning

INDEX

After the Birth of Our Child ∾ 70

A Berakah ∾ 82

Blessing Our Home ∾ 34

Blessing the New Year ∾ 39

Christ in My Spouse ∾ 50

Christmas ∾ 38

Difficulty With In-laws ∾ 65

During an Illness ∾ 59

Easter ∾ 41

An Expectant Mother's Prayer ∾ 68

A Father-to-Be's Prayer ∾ 69

For a Sick Child ∾ 74

For Family ∾ 52

For Forgiveness After an Argument ∾ 58

For Friends ∾ 51

For Patience ∾ 60

For the Friendship of My Spouse ∾ 54

For the Gift of Being Loved ∾ 48

For the Joy of Making Love ∾ 47

How Do I Love Thee?∾ 88

Job Stress ∾ 61

The Lord's Prayer for Couples ∾ 84

Love Comes From God ∾ 26

Love Does Not End ∾ 28

A Meal Blessing for Special Occasions ∾ 36

A Moment's Indulgence ∾ 87

Money Problems ∾ 62

Moving to a New Place ∾ 64

Nothing Can Come Between Us ∾ 30

Our Anniversary ∾ 43

Our Rings ∾ 19

Our Vows ∾ 18

Our Wedding Blessing ∾ 20

Our Wedding Candle ∾ 21

A Parent's Prayer ∾ 72

A Parent's Prayer for Letting Go ∾ 76

Paul's Prayer ∾ 83

Psalm 23 ∾ 81

The Season of Lent ∾ 40

Thanksgiving Day Blessing ∾ 37

Thanksgiving for Thoughtfulness ∾ 55

A Time for Everything ∾ 80

Unexpected Discoveries ∾ 46

An Unexpected Pregnancy ∾ 71

When Parenting Is Difficult ∾ 75

When We're Apart ∾ 63

Wherever You Go ∾ 24

You and I ∾ 86